Chinese Stories Book 1

for Beginners with Pinyin, English and Audio

Hong Meng 鴻蒙

Table of Contents

Introduction

This book is perfect for beginners who want to enhance their reading skills. There are 20 simple and easy to read short stories for absolute beginners who just started to learn Chinese.

The Chinese language has 4 tones and a silent tone and it consists of hundreds of thousands of words. Therefore, a better way to learn Chinese is to read and listen more.

The Pinyin is placed on top of the Chinese characters. Together with our audio files, you will be able to speed up your learning in an enjoyable way.

There are many Chinese idioms used in the stories. This will enhance your understanding on how and when the idioms are used.

The link to download all the audio files is at the end of the book.

【1】 爷爷是我最喜欢的人

我 爷爷 退休 前 是 一 位 医生。爷爷 的 头发 白白 的，眼睛 很 小，圆圆 的 脸。退休 后，他 仍然 喜欢 帮助 别人，邻里 间 也 处 得 很 好。

记得 一个 大雪 纷飞 的 夜晚，我 和 爷爷 正 坐 在 电视机 前 看《 红楼梦 》。楼下 的 张 爷爷 急匆匆 地 跑来 敲门 说："李 医生，我 老伴儿 生病 了，你 能 去 看看 吗?" 张 爷爷 的 脸 上 充满了 焦虑 和 急切。爷爷 一 听，连 鞋子 也 没 顾 得 换上 ， 穿着 拖鞋 就 往 楼下 张 爷爷 家 跑。我 怕 爷爷 一 着急 摔倒 了，也 跟着 跑了 出去。

一 进门 就 见 张 奶奶 仰面 躺 在 沙发 上，手 捂着 肚子，双眼 紧闭，眉头 皱 在 一起，

脸色 苍白，还 不时 发出 呻吟声 。 爷爷 仔细 询问了 情况，立刻 做了 简单 的 处理。 随后 让 张 爷爷 叫了 辆 车，送 张 奶奶 到 医院 的 急救 中心 去 抢救。 医生们 忙活了 好一会儿，张 奶奶 才 慢慢 地 苏醒 过来。 当 得知 时 爷爷 及时 送 她 到 医院 抢救，才 使 她 脱离了 危险 时，张 奶奶 伸出 双手 紧紧 握住 爷爷 的 手，激动 万分，连 一 句 话 也 说不出 来 了。 张 爷爷 在 一 旁 说："远亲不如近邻，真 是 太 谢谢 你 了!"爷爷 微微 一 笑 说："大伙儿 都 是 邻居，应该 互相帮助 。 何况 我 又 是 医生，就 别 客气 了。"

爷爷 这 种 助人为乐 的 精神 深深 感动了 我。 我 真的 很 喜欢 我 的 爷爷。

10

[1] English Translation

Grandpa is My Favorite Person

My grandpa was a doctor before he retired. Grandpa's hair is white; his eyes are small, his face round. When he retired, he still liked to help others, and the neighbourhood was very close.

I remember one snowy night, my grandpa and I were sitting in front of the TV watching "Dream of the Red Mansions". Grandpa Zhang from downstairs hurriedly ran to knock on the door and said, "Dr Li, my wife is ill, can you go and see her?" Grandpa Zhang's face was filled with anxiety and urgency. Grandpa did not even bother to put his shoes on, wore his slippers and ran downstairs to Grandpa Zhang's house. I was afraid grandpa would fall down the stairs, so I ran out and followed him.

As soon as I entered the door, I saw Grandma Zhang lying on the sofa with her hands on her stomach, her eyes closed, her brows frowning together, pale and groaning from time to time. Grandpa carefully checked on her and immediately performed a simple treatment. Then he asked Grandpa Zhang to call for a cab, sent Grandma Zhang to the hospital's emergency room. The doctors were busy for a while and then Grandma Zhang slowly regains her consciousness. When she learned that grandpa had sent her to the hospital just in time to rescue her from critical danger, Grandmother Zhang stretched out her hands to hold grandpa's hand, so excited that can't even say a word. Grandpa Zhang said: "Far relatives are not as good as neighbours, thank you very much!" Grandpa smiled and said, "We are all neighbours and should help each other. Besides, I'm also a doctor, so no worries. "

Grandpa's spirit of helping people has touched me deeply. Grandpa is my favourite person.

【2】 难忘的一件事

今年 暑假，我 去 乡下 舅舅 家 住了 半个 月，遇到了 一 件 事 令 我 至今 难忘 。

一 天，我 随 表 弟 去 河滩 打 猪 草，忽见 一只 喜鹊 停 在 前边 不远 的 地方。 表 弟 将 手 中了 喜鹊 的 翅膀 。 那 喜鹊 拖着 受伤 的 翅膀， 挣扎着 仓皇 逃跑。 表 弟 快步 上前， 只 一 扑，喜鹊 便 成了 他 手 中 的 俘虏。 我 上前 看 那 喜鹊，它 瞪着 眼，敲 起 嘴 "叽 叽 叽" 地 叫着， 像 在 质问 我们："我 没有 得 罪 你们，你们 为什么 要 伤害 我？我 没有 罪，为什么 要 捉 我。。。。"

那 天，我 对 表 弟 说："小弟，喜鹊 时 益鸟， 应该 保护。。。"

"什么 益鸟 不 益鸟, 我 不懂!"他 一 句 话 把 我 顶了 回来。

我 像 被人 揪了 一 把 似得 吃了 一 惊, 在 一 想, 不 只是 表弟, 一定 还有 很 多 其他 人 也 不 "懂"。他们 不仅 不懂, 还 不愿 懂。后来 我们 回 到了 家, 我 找 舅舅 帮忙, 才 解救了 这 只 受伤 得 喜鹊。

这 件 事 虽然 已 过去 很 长 时间 了, 我 却 至今 难忘。 每当 想起, 心 似乎 都 要 呐喊: 请 保护 益鸟!

[2] English Translation

An Extraordinary Thing

Last summer, I stayed at my uncle's country house for half a month, encountered an extraordinary thing.

One day, I went with my little cousin brother to the riverside to with the ragweed, suddenly saw a magpie not far away from us. My little cousin brother took the wings of the magpie in his hands. The magpie pulled his wounded wings and struggled to escape. It took a step forward, only a step, and my little cousin brother captured the magpie with his hand. I went over to see the magpie, it stared back, as if asking us: "I have not offended you, why do you hurt me?" I have no sin; why should I be caught... "

That day, I said to my little cousin brother, "Little brother, magpie should be protected... "

"What magpie? I don't understand!" he said and left me with no words.

After I overcame my shock, I thought to myself; it will not only be my little cousin brother, there must be many other people who do not "understand". Not only do they not understand, but they also don't want to. When we went home, I asked my uncle for help to save the injured magpie.

Although it has been a long time, I still can't forget this incident. Whenever I think of it, my heart seems to cry: Please protect the bird!

【3】我的家人

我的爸爸是一位老师。他中等个子，有一点儿胖，鼻梁上架着一副黑框眼镜。他在学校教地理，这副眼镜帮助他看到了中国，美国，看到了全世界。他也教历史，这副眼镜有帮助他看到了书中古今中外的历史人物，了解了变化万千的社会。爸爸的眼镜可真像一个望远镜呀！我在给爸爸画像时就画了一副大大的黑框眼镜，在镜片上还画上很多圈圈，这样就不用话爸爸的眼睛了。

妈妈呢，是一头"牛"，整天任劳任怨地干活。每天看着干净整齐的房间，吃着美味可口的饭菜，我就会情不自禁的对妈妈

15

说:"谢谢 亲爱 的 '牛' 妈妈。" 提起 妈妈 的 牛脾气,我 和 爸爸 都 没 少 领教。 有 一 次,我 睡不着午觉, 悄悄 打开 电视机, 想 轻松 一下, 却 遭到了 妈妈 严厉 的 批评。

外公 呢, 每天 早晨 总要 在 屋子 里 转圈 。 刚 开始,他 挂着 一 根 木 拐棍 和 一 根 铁拐棍 在 屋子 里 " 咣当 , 咣当 " 地 走,一会儿 又 挂着 一 副 双拐 " 咚咚 , 咚咚 " 地 走。 又 过了 一会儿,他 挂着 一 根 长 木棍 "嘟嘟,嘟嘟" 地 走。。。 不 知道 我 和 外公 整天 换 拐棍 到底 累 不 累! 真 让 人 琢磨 不透。

我 的 奶奶 是 一个 非常 勤劳 的 人,她 已经 八十多 岁 了,黑瘦 的 脸 上 布满了 皱纹, 透过

银边 老花眼镜 可以 看见 奶奶那 双 和蔼的 眼睛。她 的 一 双 小脚 走 起 路来 颤颤巍巍 的，好像 一不小心 就 会 摔倒 。她 的 手上 结满了 又 厚 又 硬 的 老茧，这 是 她 一辈子 参加 劳动 的 证明 。奶奶 的 穿着 很 俭朴，粗布 衣服 上 唯一 的 " 装饰 " 就是 那 别在 胸 前 的 一 根 闪亮 的 针，针鼻 上 还 挂着 花花绿绿 的 线头 呢。

[3] English Translation

My Family Members

My father is a teacher. He is medium size, a little fat, wears a pair of black-framed glasses on his nose. He taught geography at school, and this pair of glasses helped him see China, America, and the world. He also taught history, and this pair of glasses enabled him to see the historical figures in the book, ancient and modern, and to understand the changing society. Father's glasses are really like a telescope! I painted a pair of big black-framed glasses when I painted a picture of my father and drew a lot of circles on the lenses so that I didn't have to say draw father's eyes.

Mom is like a "cow", works all day. Looking at the clean and tidy rooms, eating delicious meals, I can't help but say to my mom: "Thank you, dear 'cow' mother." Talk about my mom's hot temper, my dad and I had quite a lot of experience. Once, I couldn't sleep at noon, quietly turned on the TV, wanted to relax, but was severely criticized by my mother.

My grandmother is a very hard-working person; she is more than eighty years old, thin black face, full of wrinkles, through the silver-edged old flower glasses, one can see grandma's kind eyes. Her little feet trembled as she walks as if she could fall anytime. Her hands were full of thick and hard callus, proof that she had been working hard all her life. Grandmother's dresses very frugally, the only "jewellery" on her is that shiny jewellery she wears on her chest, the pin with green flower.

【4】 做番茄炒蛋

今天，我决定 向 妈妈 学习 做 一 道 我 最 喜欢
的 菜 – 番茄炒蛋 。

首先 ，我 把 洗 好 的 番茄 切 正 一 小块 一
小块 的，再 分别 把 三 个 鸡蛋 轻轻 的 敲开
一条 缝，让 蛋 请和 蛋黄 流进 碗 里，并用
打蛋器 搅拌 均匀 。 搅着 搅着，一不小心，蛋清
和 蛋黄 就 溅 到 了 我 的 手上 ，感觉 凉丝丝
的, 黏糊糊 的 。 看来， 想要 做好 一 件 事,必须
仔细 才 行 呀!

接着，在 妈妈 的 指导 下,我 把 油 倒入 锅 里
烧热， 看着 冒烟 的 油,我 觉得 很 害怕,但 在
妈妈 的 不断 鼓励下,我 试着 把 搅拌 好 的 蛋
液 倒了 进去。 哇,蛋 液 膨胀 起来 了， 真像

19

一朵 美丽 的 黄色 花。我 再 也 不 害怕 了，把
"小花" 翻炒了 几 下，让 它们 分开，然后 把
番茄 倒入 锅 里 炒，放了 少许 盐，翻炒 均匀
后 就 盛 到 盘子 里。

我 迫不及待 地 端着 我 第一 次 做 的 番茄炒蛋
给 爸爸 妈妈 看。爸爸 尝了 一 口 说："这个 菜
有 一 种 幸福 的 味道!"我 听 了，心中 像
吃了 蜜 一样 甜。

[4] English Translation

Tomato Scrambled Eggs

Today, I decided to learn from my mom how to make one of my favourite dishes; tomato scrambled eggs.

First, I cut the washed tomatoes into small pieces, then tap each of the three eggs to open a seam, let the egg and yolk flow into the bowl, and use the beater to stir evenly. I stirred careless caused the egg whites and yolks to splash on my hands, immediately felt a cool sticky feeling. It seems that to do a good job, you must be careful while doing it!

Under my mom's guidance, I poured the oil into the pot to heat, I was very afraid as there was a lot of smoke, but with my mom's constant encouragement, I tried to stir the egg. Wow, the egg is swelling, it's like a beautiful yellow flower. I'm not afraid any more, I stirred the "little flowers" a few times, and then pour the tomatoes into the pot to fry, put a little salt, stir evenly and then put them on the plate.

I can't wait to let mom and dad taste my first tomato scrambled eggs. Dad tasted a mouthful and said: "This dish has a happy taste!" My heart was as sweet as honey as I heard this.

【5】窗外雨景

今天　上午，我　正在　窗　边　写　作业。　突然
看见　玻璃　花　了。　呀，原来　是　下雨　了！

我　急忙　透过　窗户　往外　看，　外面
白茫茫　一　片，模模糊糊　的，只　听见　雨声
"　刷刷　"　的　在　响　。

我　打开　窗户，雨景　清晰　多　了。　只见　雨珠
整齐　地　连了　起来，　像　是　在　空中　挂　满了
珠帘　。

我　往　楼下　瞧　去，看见　路上　盛开了　一朵朵
的　花儿。　仔细　一　瞧，哈哈，那是　一　把把　小　伞！
瞧，那不是　胖　胖　的懒羊　羊　坐在伞　上
吗？它淋　着雨，还闭着　眼睛　打瞌睡　呢！

Yǔ zhōng de jǐngsè zhēn shì tài yǒu yìsi le
雨中的景色真是太有意思了。

[5] English Translation

The Rain Scenery Outside the Window

I was doing my homework by the window this morning. Suddenly I saw the glass was blurred. Yes, it was raining!

I hurried to the window to look out; outside was white and fuzzy, can only hear the sound of the rain, "brush, brush" sound.

I opened the window and can see the rain much clearer. I saw the raindrops neatly connected as if bead curtains covering the air.

I looked downstairs and saw a flower blooming by the road. As I looked more carefully, haha, I saw that's a small umbrella! Look, isn't that a fat lazy sheep sitting on an umbrella? It's raining, and still dozing off with its eyes closed!

The view of the rain is fascinating.

【6】 暴力妹妹

我 的 妹妹 可是 一个 名副其实 的 "暴力" 女孩，什么，你 不 信？那 就 来 听 我 讲 几 个 事例 吧！

有 一 次，妈妈 到 集市 上 买了 几 个 鸡腿，做 给 我们 吃。我 和 妹妹 一人 分 到 三 个，可 妹妹 觉得 我 的 鸡腿 比 她 的 大 得 多，于是 就 说："哥哥，你 的 鸡腿 比 我 的 大，所以 必须 分给 我 一个 才 行！" 我 不肯，她 就 过来 抢 。最后，硬是 抢去了 一个，气 得 我 在 角落 里 "呜呜" 的 哭。

还 有 一 次，我 正在 看 漫画书，突然 她 无缘无故 地 跑 过来 推了 我 一 把，我 火 了，说了 她 一 句，谁知，她 就 跑到 外面 去 哭，哭着 哭着 竟然 坐 到 地上 了，又 哭了 一会儿，干脆

就 在 地上 睡着 了。 这 是，妈妈 过来 了，好不容易 才 把 妹妹 从 地上 给 抱了 起来。

这 就是 我 的 "暴力" 妹妹，我 很 喜欢 她，你 呢？

[6] English Translation

My Violent Sister

My sister is a veritable "violent" girl. You don't believe me? Then let me tell you a few examples!

Once, my mother went to the market to buy a few chicken legs to cook for us to eat. My sister and I each has three chicken legs, but my sister thought the chicken legs I have are much bigger than the ones she has, so she said: "Brother, your chicken legs are bigger than mine, so you must give me a one!" Of course I won't; anyhow she just came and grabbed it from me. Finally, she managed to grab it from me and I was so angry that I stood at the corner and cried.

Another time, I was reading a comic book, suddenly she ran over for no reason and pushed me, I was so angry I scolded her badly, she ran outside to cry, sat on the floor and cried. After a while, she simply fell asleep on the floor. Then, mother came over and picked her up from the floor. It was not easy for mother to carry my sister .

This is my "violent" sister, I like her very much, what about you?

【7】雪

Xuěhuā fēnfēn-yángyáng piāopiāo sǎsǎ de cóngtiān'érjiàng
雪花 纷纷扬扬，飘飘 洒洒 地 从天而降，

tāmen xiàng yígègè kě'ài de jīnglíng yòu hǎoxiàng shì xiānnǚ
他们 像 一个个可爱的 精灵，又 好像 是 仙女

sònggěi dōngtiān de lǐwù
送给 冬天 的 礼物。

Xuěhuā fēi dào le xióngzhuàng de gāoshān gēge de jiān
雪花 飞 到了 雄壮 的 高山 哥哥 的 肩

shàng shì gāoshān gēge biànde gèng jiā yǒu mèilì le
上，是 高山 哥哥 变得 更 家 有 魅力 了。

Xuěhuā piāo dào le ài dǎban dìdì shù mèimei shēnshang
雪花 飘 到了 爱 打扮 的的 树 妹妹 身上，

sònggěi shù mèimei yì píng xuěhuā rùnfū shuāng shǐ shù
送给 树 妹妹 一 瓶 雪花 润肤 霜，使 树

mèimei gèngjiā kě'ài mírén Xuěhuā tiào dào le lǎoshi de
妹妹 更加 可爱 迷人。 雪花 跳 到了 老实 的

xiǎomài dìdì shēnshang wèi zhèng dòng dé sèsè fādǒu de
小麦 弟弟 身上，为 正 冻 得 瑟瑟 发抖 的

xiǎomài dìdi gàishang yì chuáng hòuhòu de miánbèi
小麦 弟弟 盖上 一 床 厚厚 的 棉被。

Xuěhuā luò dào le cíxiáng de dàdì mǔqin de huáibào lǐ wèi
雪花 落 到了 慈祥 的 大地 母亲 的 怀抱 里，为

dàdì mǔqin pīshàng yí jiàn jiébái de yīshang
大地 母亲 披上 一 件 洁白 的 衣裳。

雪 停 了，人们 在 雪地 上 留下 的 脚印 就 像 一串串 和谐 美好 的 音符，它们 演奏 出了 这 一 首 冬 填 的 赞歌。我 朝 四周 望了 望，没有 人 扫 雪，可能 是 人们 不 想 破坏者 美好 的 景色 吧。

雪！你 是 冬天 的 精灵，装饰了 这个 世界。

雪，我 爱 你。

[7] English Translation

Snow

Snowflakes are rising, floating from the sky, they are like a lovely elf, but also like a fairy to the gift of winter.

Snowflakes flew over the shoulders of the majestic mountain brother, who became more attractive at home. Snowflakes fell on the tree sister who loved to dress up, and gave the tree sister a bottle of snowflake moisturiser, making the tree sister more lovely and charming. Snowflakes jumped on the honest wheat brother, covering the frozen wheat brother with a bed of thick cotton. Snowflakes fell into the arms of the kind mother of the earth, for the mother of the earth put on a white dress.

The snow stopped, and the footprints left on the snow were like a string of harmonious notes, and they played the song of winter. I looked around, no one swept the snow, maybe people don't want to spoil the beautiful scenery.

Snow! You are the elf of winter, decorating the world. Snow, I love you.

【8】 踢足球

Jīntiān wǒ zàijiā mēnle yì tiān māma shuō wǒ kěyǐ xiàlóu tòu
今天 我 在家 闷了 一 天，妈妈 说 我 可以 下楼 透
tòuqì yùndòng yùndòng huì gǎnjué shūfu yìxiē
透气，运动 运动，会 感觉 舒服 一些。

Yúshì wǒ jiù bàozhe zúqiú xiàlóu zhǎo dào le xiǎo huǒbàn
于是，我 就 抱着 足球 下楼，找 到了 小 伙伴
wáng xīn yǔ zhǔnbèi lái yì chǎng èr rén duìkàngsài
王 心 雨，准备 来一 场 "二人 对抗赛"。

Bǐsài kāishǐ le wǒ dì-yī ge chōngguò duìfāng fángxiàn jìnle
比赛 开始 了，我 第一 个 冲过 对方 防线，进了
yì qiú Wáng xīn yǔ kàn wǒ xiànzài de qiújì jìnbù hěn dà
一 球。 王 心 雨 看 我 现在 的 球技 进步 很 大，
biànshì chūle kānjiāběnlǐng Zhǐjiàn tā láile ge shén lóng
便是 出了 看家本领 。 只见 他 来了 个 神 龙
bǎiwěi wǒ yǐ wéi tā huì bǎ qiú xiǎng wǒ yòubian tī méi
摆尾，我 以 为 他 会 把 球 想 我 右边 踢，没
xiǎngdào tā què tūrán cóng wǒ zuǒbian jiāng qiú tī jìnle
想到 他 却 突然 从 我 左边 将 球 踢 进了
qiúmén Wǒ dāngrán méiyǒu dǎngzhù hái chàdiǎn shuāile yì
球门 。 我 当然 没有 挡住，还 差点 摔了 一
jiāo dòu dé tā yǎnlèi dōu xiàole chūlái
跤，逗 得 他 眼泪 都 笑了 出来。

我们 就 这样 激战了 半 小时 左右，浑身上下 都 被 汗水 湿透 了，也 没 分出 胜负 来。

王 心 雨，下次 我 一定 要 踢过 你， 哼哼 ！

[8] English Translation

Play Football

Today, I was at home for a day, my mother said I could go downstairs breath a little and exercise, I will feel more comfortable.

So, I took the football with me downstairs, found little partner, Wang Xinyu, ready to play a "two-man match."

The game started, and I was the first to crossed the defence line and scored a goal. Wang Xinyu saw that my current game skills had improved a lot, that is, out of the housekeeping skills. I saw him coming, I thought he would kick the ball to my right, but he suddenly kicked the ball to my left into the goal post. Of course, I didn't block it. I almost fell, and he laughed until his tears rolled out.

We were played hard for about half an hour, and our bodies were soaked with sweat, and yet no one wins the game.

Wang Xinyu, I must beat you next time, hehe!

【9】 我说你做

今天 我们 做了 一个 叫 "我 说 你 做" 的 有趣
游戏,游戏 的 要求 是 表演 老师 说 的 内容。

一 开始,老师 说出 一个 词:"举手",有的 同学
很 快 举起 了手,有的 却 还 呆呆 的 坐 在 那里。

接着,老师 又 说:"捏 左 耳朵,捏 左 耳朵!" 哇!
大家 急忙 去 捏 左 耳朵,动作 非常 混乱。"捏
右 耳朵,捏 右 耳朵!" 同学们 都 乱 成
一锅粥。" 方向 ! 右边 ! 右边 !不,是 左边 !
左边 !" 有的 同学 傻笑 起来, 活像 一个 疯子。
过了 好一会 儿,大家 的 动作 才 变得 整齐划一 。

这个 游戏 真 是 太 有趣 了,你 说 呢?

[9] English Translation

I Say You Do It

Today we played a fun game called "I say you do it". The requirement of the game is we perform what the teacher said.

At first, the teacher said: "put up your hand", some students quickly raised their hands, and some still sat there and didn't do anything.

Then, the teacher said: "Pinch the left ear, pinch the left ear!" "Wow! Everyone rushed to pinch their left ears; the movement was very chaotic. "Pinch your right ear, pinch your right ear!" The students were all very chaotic like a pot of mashed up porridge. "Direction! Right! Right! No, it's the left! Left!" Some students giggled and laughed like a madman. After a while, everyone's movements became uniform.

This game was so exciting, don't you think?

【10】小鸡的脸红了

一个 阳光明媚 的 早晨，小鸡 看到 头顶 上 金黄 的 太阳，懒 懒 地 说："今天 的 阳光 真 好，我 要 好好 地 享受 阳光浴 。"

小鸡 躺 在 草地 上 ， 正 享受 这 暖 暖 的 阳光 。 突然，它 听到 小猪 的 声音："小鸡，别 晒太阳 了，快 来 帮 我 盖房子 吧!" 小鸡 说："不干 不干，盖房子 又 脏 又 费 力气，我 要 在 这儿 晒太阳 。" 小鸡 的 话音 刚 落，他 又 听到了 小鸭 的 声音："小鸡，快 来 帮 我 磨 面 吧!" 小鸡 又 说："不干 不干，磨 面 太 累 了，我 在 享受 阳光浴 呢!"

下午，忽然 下起了 大雨，小鸡 的 房子 楼宇 了，小鸡 拿来 水桶，脸盆 接雨。 小猪 和 小鸭 看见 了，赶紧 过来 帮 小鸡 把 房子 修好 了。

小鸡 看到 修好 的 房子，再 看看 浑身湿透 了 地 小猪 和 小鸭，不 好意思 地 低下了 头。 小猪 说："大家 相互 帮助 是 应该 的。"这时，小鸡 的 脸红 红 的，像 一个 红 苹果 。

从此，小鸡 也 变得 乐于助人 了。

[10] English Translation

The Chicken's Face is Red

One sunny morning, the chicken saw the golden sun on the top of his head, lying lazily: "Today's sunshine is very good. I want to enjoy sunbath." "

The chicken was lying on the grass, enjoying the warm sun. Suddenly, it heard the piglet's voice: "Chicken, don't bask in the sun, come and help me build a house!" The chicken said, "I don't want to do it, building a house is dirty and requires hard work. I'm going to bask in the sun here." The chicken's voice just stopped. It then heard the duckling's voice: "Chicken, come and help me grind the surface!" The chicken added: "I don't want to do, grinding the surface is too tiring, I am enjoying the sunbath!" "

In the afternoon, suddenly it began to rain heavily, the chicken's house was leaking, the chicken used buckets and basins to catch the rain. The piglet and duckling saw this, hurried over to help the chicken fix the house.

The chicken saw the repaired house, and then looked at the wet piglet and duckling, embarrassed with his head bowed. "It's the right thing to do to help each other, " said the piglet. At this time, the chicken's face was so red, as red as an apple.

From then on, the chicken became helpful.

【11】登泰山

周末，我和爸爸妈妈一起去泰山游玩。经过五个多小时的车程，我们终于来到了太山脚下。我们是坐索道上山的，那种感觉就像飞起来一样。

山上的风景很美，有各种各样的树，五彩缤纷的花。它们在山风的吹拂下招着小手，好像在欢迎我们这些远道而来的游客。山中还有各种奇形怪状的石头，有的石头上刻着大字，有的石头上刻着诗歌。听爸爸讲，这些刻在山石上的字大部分都是古代文人墨客游泰山时留下的感慨。我边走边拿着相机不停地拍照。

继续往上走就是"玉皇顶"了。那美丽的霞光和绿树、红墙、黄瓦相互辉映，给泰山增添了不少诗情画意。我站在瞭望石上高喊："我来了！"声音传到远方，产生了阵阵回音。周围的人看见我在喊，也都大声呼喊。

泰山给我留下了美好的回忆，也给我带来了登顶的成就感。

[11] English Translation

Taishan

During the weekend, I went to Taishan with my parents. After more than five hours of driving, we finally arrived at the foot of Taishan. We took the cable car up the mountain; it felt as if we were flying up.

The scenery at the top of the mountain is beautiful, with all kinds of trees and colourful flowers. They were dancing under the breeze of the mountain as if they were welcoming us from afar. There are also a variety of strange-shaped stones on the mountain. Some of the stones were engraved with Chinese characters, and some were engraved with Chinese poems. Dad said that most of the words carved on the rocks were engraved by ancient literati when they visited Taishan. I kept taking pictures with my camera while walking.

We went up to the "Jade Emperor's Top". That beautiful light and green trees, red walls, yellow tiles reflecting each other, added much poetic meaning to Taishan. I stood on the watch-stone and shouted, "I'm coming!" The sound travelled far and produced a burst of echo. People around saw me shouting, and they started to do the same.

Taishan left me a good memory and brought me a sense of accomplishment.

【12】呆爸爸

Wǒ bàba zhēn dāi xiànzài jiù ràng wǒ jièshào yíxià wǒ de
我 爸爸 真 "呆",现在 就 让 我 介绍 一下 我 的
dāi bàba ba
呆 爸爸 吧!

　　Háizi tā bàba kuàidiǎn lái bāngmáng xǐ dòujiǎo Zài
"孩子 他 爸爸, 快点 来 帮忙 洗 豆角!" 在
chúfáng lǐ mánglù de māma dàshēng hǎnzhe kě bàba hái
厨房 里 忙碌 的 妈妈 大声 喊着,可 爸爸 还
shì wénsī-búdòng de zuò zài diànshìjī qián Ài Wǒ gāng
是 纹丝不动 地 坐 在 电视机 前。 "唉!" 我 刚
tànle kǒuqì māma jiù chōng le guòlai buguò bàba hái shì
叹了 口气,妈妈 就 冲 了 过来,不过 爸爸 还 是
yíyàng dāi zuò zài diànshìjī qián
一样 呆 坐 在 电视机 前。

Yǒu yì tiān wǒ zài shāngdiàn lǐ kànshangle yí ge liǎng yuán
有 一 天,我 在 商店 里 看上了 一个 两 元
qián de xiǎowányìr jiù chánzhe bàba yào tā mǎi tā hěn
钱 的 小玩意儿,就 缠着 爸爸 要 他 买,他 很
kuài jiù dāying le Dào yàoqián shí bàba tāochū yìzhāng
快 就 答应 了。 到 要钱 时,爸爸 掏出 一张 10
yuán de chāopiào dìgěi shōuyínyuán hòu hái méi děng
元 的 钞票,递给 收银员 后,还 没 等
zhǎoqián jiù wǎngwài zǒu māma yì bǎ zhuāzhù bàba de
找钱 就 往外 走,妈妈 一 把 抓住 爸爸 的
shǒu shuō Nǐ xiǎng shénme ne Bú yàoqián le
手 说:"你 想 什么 呢? 不 要钱 了?"

春节 前一天，爸爸 带 我 到 公园 玩，我 尽情 地 把 娱乐 项目 玩了 个 痛快，可 爸爸 却 不 玩，只是 呆呆 地 站 在 外面，看着 我 傻笑。回家 的 途中，突然 刮起了 大风，我 说："好 冷 呀!" 爸爸 马上 脱下 她、他 的 棉衣 披 在 我 身上 。

瞧，我 爸爸 够 "呆" 吧? 我 爱 我 的 呆爸爸!

[12] English Translation

Foolish Dad

My dad really "foolish", let me introduce my daddy now!

"Child, his father, hurry up come help me wash the beans!", my busy mother shouted from the kitchen, but Dad didn't move and still sat in front of the TV. "Alas! As soon as I sighed, my mother rushed over, but Dad sat in front of the TV.

One day, I saw a two-yuan gadget in the store, and I pestered my father to buy it, and he quickly agreed. When he was asked to pay, Dad took out a 10 yuan bill and handed it to the cashier. He left the store without waiting for the change. Mother grabbed my father's hand and said, "What are you thinking? Don't you want the change?"

One day before the Spring Festival, my father took me to the park to play. I enjoyed playing at the park with great pleasure, but my father didn't join me, he just stood there and giggled. On the way home, suddenly there was a gust of strong wind. I said, "It's so cold!" Dad immediately took off his cotton coat and put it on me.

Hey, my dad is foolish enough? But I love my daddy very much!

【13】 第一次包饺子

Jīntiān jiā lǐ chī jiǎozi wǒ hái cóng méiyǒu zìjǐ bāoguo
今天 家 里 吃 饺子，我 还 从 没有 自己 包过
jiǎozi yúshì jiù kuài dìngxiàng māma qǐngjiào yíxià bāojiǎozi
饺子，于是 就 快 定向 妈妈 请教 一下 包饺子
de fāngfǎ
的 方法。

Māma ràng wǒ xiān bǎ zìjǐ de shǒu xǐ gānjìng Děng wǒ
妈妈 让 我 先 把 自己 的 手 洗 干净。 等 我
de shǒu xǐ gānjìng hòu māma jiù ràng wǒ bǎ róuhǎo de
的 手 洗 干净 后，妈妈 就 让 我 把 揉好 的
yìtuán miàn qiēchéng sān fèn Qiè hǎo hòu māma ràng wǒ bǎ
一团 面 切成 三 份。切 好 后，妈妈 让 我 把
měi yí fèn dōu cuō chéng xiǎo tiáotiáo yòng dāo bǎ měi yí ge
每 一 份 都 搓 成 小 条条，用 刀 把 每 一个
xiǎo tiáotiáo dōu qiēchéng xiǎo miàntuán zài ràng wǒ bǎ tāmen
小 条条 都 切成 小 面团，再 让 我 把 它们
dōu àn chéng xiǎo bǐng zuìhòu zuòchéng jiǎozi pí Jiēxiàlái
都 按 成 小 饼，最后 做成 饺子 皮。接下来，
wǒ zé jìxù àn māma jiāo wǒ de fāngfǎ bāojiǎozi Xiān bǎ
我 则 继续 按 妈妈 教 我 的 方法 包饺子。 先 把
jiǎozi pí fàng zài zuǒshǒu shàng ránhòu yòng sháozi wāle yì
饺子 皮 放 在 左手 上，然后 用 勺子 挖了 一
sháo jiǎozixiàn fàng zài jiǎozi zhōngjiān bǎ jiǎozi pí xiàng nèi
勺 饺子馅 放 在 饺子 中间，把 饺子 皮 向 内
zhé liǎngxià zhé chū liǎng ge tūchū lái de yìnjì hòu zài bǎ
折 两下，折 出 两 个 突出 来 的 印记 后，再 把

饺子皮的交叉口使劲的捏几下。就这样，一个饺子就完成了。我按照这个程序，很快就包了十几个饺子！

第一次包饺子，我真的好开心！

[13] English Translation

Making Dumplings for the First Time

Today, we are going to have dumplings at home. I have never wrapped dumplings before, so I asked my mom how to make dumplings.

Mom asked me to wash my hands first. After I cleaned my hands, my mom asked me to cut the dough into three. After cutting it, my mom asked me to cut each piece into small strips, then cut each small strip into a small dough with a knife, and then asked me to press them into small cakes, and finally made the dumpling skin. Next, I continued to make dumplings according to the way my mom taught me. First, put the dumpling skin on the left hand, then use a spoon to dig a spoonful of dumpling filling and place it in the middle of the dumpling skin, fold the dumplings inward twice, fold out the two prominent marks, and then make the intersection of the dumplings hard. Pinch it a few times, and the dumpling is finished. I followed this procedure and soon packed more than a dozen dumplings!

I was really pleased to make dumplings for the first time!

【14】笑掉牙

期末考试的 前一天，我 吃完 晚饭 后，奶奶 亲切
地 对我 说："小 王， 明天 就要 考试 了，你
只要 认真 做题，数学 和 英语 一定 能考 一
百分，语文 就考 个 九十五 分 吧。"我 信心十足 地
说："没 问题。 语文 我 也要 考 一 百分 呢!"
奶奶 笑着 说："那 我 就要 笑 掉 牙 了!"

我 想：奶奶 笑 掉 牙还 怎么 吃饭 呢？这 可不
行。 于是，我 风趣 地 说："为了 不让 奶奶 笑
掉 牙，我 就考 个 九十五 分 吧!"

爷爷 听了 我俩 的 对话 "哈哈" 笑了 起来，奶奶 和
我 也 跟着 笑 了，屋子 里 充满了 欢笑声 。

[14] English Translation

Laughing Off Your Teeth

The day before the final exam, after I finished dinner, my grandmother said to me kindly: "Little Wang, you will be sitting for your exam tomorrow, just focus and concentrate, for maths and English you will be able to get a full 100 points, and as for Chinese language test you will be able to get 95 points." I said confidently, "No problem. I also want to get a 100 points for the Chinese test!" Grandma smiled and said, "Then I'm going to laugh off my teeth!" "

I thought to myself: "If Grandma laughs off her teeth, how is she going to eat?" That's not going to work. So, I said humorously: "In order not to let Grandma's teeth fall off, I will get 95 points!" "

Grandpa listened to our dialogue and laughed, Grandma and I also laughed and filled the room with laughter.

【15】 上课铃响了

"丁铃铃"，上课铃响了，同学们争先恐后地冲进教室，沸腾的小园顿时安静下来。小月同学坐在座位上一边喘着粗气，一边飞快地从书包里拿出书本放在桌角上，然后端端正正的坐好；"小不点儿"急忙咽下嘴里的面包，赶紧挺直身体。李老师像往常一样夹着书本微笑着站在门口环视全班同学。刹那间，教室里鸦雀无声。只见李老师步履轻快地走上讲台，放下书本，从粉笔盒里拿出一根粉笔，转身在黑板上写了起来。

这节课就这样开始了。

[15] English Translation

The Class Bell Rang

"Ding lingling", the class bell rang, and the students rushed into the classroom, and the school garden suddenly calmed down. Xiaoyue, sat in her seat while gasping for air, she quickly took a book out of the bag and put it at the corner of the table, and then sat upright and then quickly sat up straight. Teacher Li stood at the door and looked around the class as usual with a book on his hand. In an instant, the classroom was silent. I saw Teacher Li walked briskly onto the podium, put the book down, took out a piece of chalk from the chalk box, and then turned and wrote on the blackboard.

The lesson began like this.

【16】淘气的弟弟

今天是星期六，妈妈把照顾小弟弟地任务交给了我，我一想起那淘气的小弟弟就很头疼。唉。。。他冲我甜甜的笑了一下，可是我怎么感觉他的笑容让我很不安呢？不管了，我还是做我的作业吧！这时，小弟弟趁我不注意，悄悄地流进了我的房间，并轻轻地关上了门。

过了一会儿，我做完了作业，伸了一个懒腰，突然听见我的房间里发出了"砰 砰砰"的声音，再走近一点儿，声音越来越大。我打开房门一看，顿时傻眼了，原本干干净净，整整齐齐的房间都被这"小 魔王"给"毁"了。我气的七窍生烟，瞪着这个"小

魔王"，他 不仅 没有 害怕，还 得 意 地 冲 我

笑， 好像 这 里面 发生 的 一切 都 与 他 无关 。

唉! 摊 上 这个 " 小 魔王 "，我 真 是 倒霉 啊!

你们 说，做 一个 合格 的 姐姐 容易 吗？

[16] English Translation

Naughty Brother

Today is Saturday; my mother gave me the task of taking care of my younger brother. When I think of the naughty little brother, and it gave me a headache. Alas, he smiled sweetly at me, but why did I feel his smile upsets me? No matter what, I still have to do my homework! While I was not paying attention, my younger brother quietly went into my room and gently closed the door.

After I finished my homework, stretched my waist, and suddenly heard a "beep" sound in my room, and when I walked closer, the sound grew louder and louder. When I opened the door and looked, I was dumbfounded. The room was so clean and neat, now "destroyed" by the "little devil." Fuming in smoke and anger, I glared at this "little devil", but he not only is not afraid but proudly smiled at me, as if everything that happened inside had nothing to do with him.

Ugh! I am unlucky to have this "little devil" as a brother! Do you think it is easy being a sister?

【17】 大脚脚和小脚脚

晚上，妈妈给我洗脚，洗的暖暖和和的，舒服极了。趁我不注意，妈妈就偷偷用手指挠我的脚底，我痒的直笑，弄得水盆里溅出了好多水花。我连忙说："妈妈，饶命！""好，我不挠你了！"妈妈嘴上答应了，可我刚放松警惕，安静下来，她又开始挠我了，还逗我说："小脚脚，小脚脚！"好像我是个小毛头似的。

等妈妈躺进被子里的时候，我决定"报复"妈妈一下，就悄悄地把冰凉凉的小手进了被子，一下子抓住了妈妈的脚，大声喊："大脚脚，大脚脚！"这下妈妈也大喊大叫起来：

"女儿，收 好 凉 啊，救命!" 然后 我们 就 笑 作 一团。

我 和 妈妈 经常 这样 闹着玩儿，你 说，我俩 像 不 像 好 朋友 呢?

[17] English Translation

Big feet and little feet

In the evening, my mother washed my feet, and the warmth of the water was very comfortable. While I wasn't paying attention, my mother secretly tickled my feet with her fingers. I was so tickled I made a lot of splashes in the bathtub. I quickly said: "Mom, please let me go!" "Okay, I will stop tickling you!" Mom promised, but as I relaxed and let my guard down, she began to tickle me again, and teased me: "Little feet , little feet!"

When my mother was lying in the quilt, I decided to "revenge" my mother, and quietly slide my cold little hands into the quilt, and suddenly grabbed the mother's foot and shouted: "Big feet, big feet!" Mother also cried: "Daughter, its very cold, help!" Then we laughed.

My mother and I often play like this. Are we not like good friends?

【18】我的生日

Jīntiān shì wǒ de shēngri wǒ yídàzǎo jiùqǐlai le Wǒ
今天 是 我 的 生日，我 一大早 就起来 了。 我
zǒudào bàba māma de fángjiān qián yí kàn mén hái guān
走到 爸爸 妈妈 的 房间 前，一 看，门 还 关
zhene
着呢!

Wǒ xīnxiǎng Bàba māma zhēn huài jīntiān wǒ guòshēngrì
我 心想："爸爸 妈妈 真 坏，今天 我 过生日，
hái bù qǐ chuáng Wǒ bùyóude shēngqì qǐlai Piānpiān zhè
还 不 起 床 。"我 不由得 生气 起来。 偏偏 这
shíhou xiǎngqǐle qiāomén shēng wǒ nùqì-chōngchōng de shuō
时候 响起了 敲门 声，我 怒气冲冲 的 说：
Shéi a Yídàzǎo jiù qiāomén Yízhèn shúxī de shēngyīn
" 谁 啊？一大早 就 敲门 !" 一阵 熟悉 的 声音
chuánlái Kāimén ya érzi
传来 :" 开门 呀, 儿子!"

Wǒ tīngdào hòu jímáng qù kāimén yuánlái shì bàba māma mǎi
我 听到 后 急忙 去 开门，原来 是 爸爸 妈妈 买
dōngxi huílái le Bàba nále yí ge sāncéng dàngāo māma
东西 回来 了。爸爸 拿了 一个 三层 蛋糕，妈妈
tízhe yì lánzi cài Wǒ dītóu kànle kàn lánzi wā jī yā yú
提着 一 篮子 菜。我 低头 看了 看 篮子, 哇, 鸡, 鸭, 鱼,
ròu yàngyàng yǒu háiyǒu wǒ zuì xǐhuan chī de pángxiè ne
肉 样样 有, 还有 我 最 喜欢 吃 的 螃蟹 呢!

Wǒ yì bǎ lǒuzhùle bàba māma duì tāmen shuō Bàba
我 一 把 搂住了 爸爸 妈妈, 对 他们 说: "爸爸

māma wǒ ài nǐmen
妈妈, 我 爱 你们!"

[18] English Translation

My Birthday

Today is my birthday, so I got up early in the morning. I went to my parents' room, and the door was still closed!

I thought to myself: "Mom and Dad are really bad. Today is my birthday, and they can't get out of bed. " I couldn't help getting angry. Then, there was a knock on the door, and I said in anger: "Who knocks on the door so early in the morning!" A familiar voice said: "Open the door, son!"

I heard that, and I rushed to open the door. It turned out that my parents were buying things. Dad was holding a three-layer cake and Mom was carrying a basket of food. I looked into the basket, wow, chicken, duck, fish, meat, and my favourite crab!

I hugged my parents and said, "Mom and Dad, I love you!"

【19】 看牙记

Qiántiān zǎoshang wǒ zhèngzài chīfàn hūrán gǎnjué yáténg
前天　早上，我　正在　吃饭，忽然 感觉 牙疼。

Wǒ lìkè pǎoqù zhào jìngzi yuánlái shì chángle yì kē zhùyá
我 立刻 跑去 照镜子，原来 是 长了 一 颗 蛀牙。

Māma zhīdao le lìkè bǎ wǒ dài dào le yīyuàn Láidào yákē
妈妈 知道 了，立刻 把 我 带 到了 医院。来到 牙科，

wǒ yìzhí wǔzhe sāibāngzi zhèshí wǒ cái tǐhuì dào diànshì
我 一直 捂着 腮帮子，这时，我 才 体会 到 电视

guǎnggào lǐ cháng shuō de yí jù huà Yáténg bú shì bìng
广告 里 常 说 的 一 句 话："牙疼 不 是 病，

téngqǐlai zhēn yàomìng Buguò zhè dōu guài wǒ zìjǐ bù tīng
疼起来 真 要命 。"不过 这 都 怪 我自己 不 听

bàba māma de huà tāmen píngshí jiù ràng wǒ shǎo chī táng
爸爸 妈妈 的 话，他们 平时 就 让 我 少 吃 糖。

Xiǎng zhuóxiǎng zhe lúndào gěi wǒ zhìliáo le wǒ xīnzhōng
想　着想　着，轮到 给 我 治疗 了，我　心中

dùnshí hàipà jíle
顿时 害怕 极了。

Yīshēng jiào wǒ zài yǐzi shàng tǎngxia zhāngdà zuǐba
医生　叫 我 在 椅子 上　躺下，张大　嘴巴，

ránhòu náchū gōngjù gěi wǒ jiǎnchá bù zhīdao yīshēng gěi wǒ
然后 拿出 工具 给 我 检查，不 知道 医生 给 我

shàngle diǎnr shénme yào kǔ dé yàomìng guòle yíhuìr wǒ
上了 点儿 什么 药，苦 得 要命，过了 一会儿，我

的牙就 没有 刚才 那么 疼 了,这 种 药水
好 神奇!

经过 这 次 牙疼 事件 后,我 再 也 不敢 吃 糖
了。 顺便 提醒 同学们 ,要 好好 的 保护 牙齿,
长 蛀牙 真 难受 哇!

[19] English Translation

Look at My Tooth

The day before yesterday, while I was eating, suddenly I felt my toothache. I immediately ran to look in the mirror, it turned out to be tooth decay.

I told my Mom, and she immediately took me to the hospital. When I went to dentistry, I have been covering my cheek. Then I realized what I often heard on TV commercials: "Toothache is not a disease, but it hurts terribly." I blame myself for not listening to my parents; they usually asked me not to eat so many sweets. As I was thinking about it, suddenly it was my turn to be treated, and I was terrified.

The doctor told me to lie down on the chair, open my mouth, and then took out some tools to check my teeth. I didn't know what medicine the doctor gave me, it was so bitter. After a while, my teeth didn't hurt so much. This potion is amazing!

After this toothache incident, I no longer dare to eat sweets. By the way, you must also protect your teeth well. Otherwise, tooth decay is uncomfortable!

【20】老鼠嫁女

很久以前，一对年迈的老鼠夫妇住在阴湿寒冷的黑洞里。看着女儿一天天长大，夫妇俩便想要为女儿找一个最好的婆家，要让女儿摆脱这种不见天日的生活。于是，老鼠夫妇便出门提亲了。

刚一出门，他们便看见天空中雄赳赳的太阳。它们琢磨着，太阳是世间最强大的，任何黑暗都惧怕太阳的光芒。女儿嫁给太阳，不就是嫁给了光明吗？太阳听了老鼠夫妇的请求，皱着眉头说："可敬的老人们，我不是你们想象的那样强壮，黑云可以遮住我的光芒。"

老鼠 夫妇 哑口无言。于是 它们 来到 黑云 哪里，向 黑云 提亲。黑云 苦笑着 回答:" 尽管 我 有 遮挡 光芒 的 力量，但是 只 需要 一丝 微风，就 可以 让 我 消失。"

老鼠 夫妇 找 到了 克制 黑云 的 风。风 笑 道:"我 可以 吹散 黑云，但是 只要 一 堵 墙 就 可以 把 我 制服!" 老鼠 夫妇 又 找到 墙，墙 看到 它们，恐惧 的 说:" 在 这个 世界 上，我 最 怕 你们 老鼠，任凭 再 坚固 的 墙 也 抵挡 不住 你们 老鼠 打 洞 啊!"

老鼠 夫妇 绵绵 相觑，心想:看来 还 是 咱们 老鼠 最 有 力量。老鼠 妈妈 说:"那 我们 老鼠 又 怕 谁 呢? 对了! 自古以来 老鼠 都

怕 猫!"于是，老鼠 夫妇 找 到了 花 猫，坚持 要
将 女儿 嫁给 花 猫。

花 猫 哈哈大笑，满口答应 了 下来。于是，老鼠
夫妇 用 最 隆重 的 仪式 送 最 美丽 的 女儿
出嫁。然而 意想不到 的 事情 发生 了，花 猫
从 背后 蹿 出来，一 口 就 吃掉 了 自己 的
新娘 。

[20] English Translation

Marrying off Mouse Daughter

A long time ago, an elderly couple of mice lived in a damp, cold black hole. As their daughter grow up day by day, the couple wanted to find the best husband for their daughter, and let her daughter be rid of this unseen life. So the mice couple went out to find a son in law.

As soon as they went out, they saw the majestic sun in the sky. They wonder the sun is the most powerful in the world, and any darkness is afraid of the sun. If the daughter is married to the sun, wouldn't she be married to the light? The sun listened to the request of the mice couple, frowned and said: "Respectable old mice, I am not as strong as you think, the dark cloud can cover my light."

The mice couple were speechless. So they went to the dark cloud. Dark Cloud smiled and replied: "Although I have the power to block the light, only a trace of breeze can make me disappear."

The mice couple found the wind that blew away the dark clouds. The wind laughed and said: "I can blow away the dark cloud, but I can be blocked by a wall!" The mice couple found the wall, and the wall said with fear: "In this world, I am most afraid of you, mice. The hardened walls could not resist the holes that the mouse make!"

The mice couple were stunned, thought to themselves: It seems that the mouse is the most powerful. The mouse mother said: "Who are we afraid? Right! Rats have been afraid of cats since ancient times!" So, the mice couple found the cat and insisted that the cat should marry their daughter.

The cat laughed and agreed to it. So the mouse couple married their beautiful daughter in a solemn ceremony. However, an unexpected thing happened, the cat came out from the back, ate his bride.

Audio Download

Link to direct download of free audio files:

https://allmusing.net/hong-meng/chinese-stories-book-1-audio/8/

Password to download the audio files:

&#UeJP95=c

Please download all the files **within 7 days** of purchase.

Printed in Poland
by Amazon Fulfillment
Poland Sp. z o.o., Wrocław

52200068R00040